DATE DUE

★ *GREAT SPORTS TEAMS* ★

THE PHOENIX

BASKETBALL TEAM

David Pietrusza

Enslow Publishers, Inc.

44 Fadem Road	PO Box 38
Box 699	Aldershot
Springfield, NJ 07081	Hants GU12 6BP
USA	UK

*Dedicated to my wife, Patty, who makes possible
the best homecourt in the league.*

Acknowledgments:

*Thanks to the public relations department of the Phoenix Suns and to
fellow Enslow Publishers author Jack Kavanagh.*

Library of Congress Cataloging-in-Publication Data

Pietrusza, David, 1949–
    The Phoenix Suns basketball team / David Pietrusza.
        p. cm. — (Great sports teams)
    Includes bibliographical references (p.) and index.
    Summary: Traces the history of the Phoenix Suns basketball team,
including major players, coaches, and playoff games.
    ISBN 0-89490-795-6
    1. Phoenix Suns (Basketball team)—History—Juvenile literature.
    [1. Phoenix Suns (Basketball team)—History. 2. Basketball—History.]
    I. Title. II. Series.
GV885.52.P47P54 1997
796.323'64'0979173—dc20   96-26412
                                                              CIP
                                                               AC

Printed in the United States of America

10 9 8 7 6 5 4 3 2 1

Illustration Credits: AP/Wide World Photos, pp. 4, 7, 8, 10, 13, 14, 16,
19, 20, 22, 25, 26, 28, 31, 32, 34, 37, 38.

Cover Illustration: AP/Wide World Photos.

CONTENTS

*D*on Nelson of Boston beats Phoenix's Garfield Heard to the loose ball. Boston and Phoenix were fighting for the 1976 NBA Championship.

THE GARDEN PARTY

There were just fifty-five seconds to go. After many frustrating years without making the playoffs, the Phoenix Suns stood on the brink of losing Game 5 of the 1975–76 NBA Finals. If the Suns lost tonight, the Boston Celtics would need just one more win to take it all. It would be no disgrace to lose to the Celtics, who had long dominated the NBA. Many other great teams had lost over the decades, but professionals are always frustrated to lose.

The Suns were a young team who had surprised everyone by making the playoffs and reaching the NBA Finals. They featured rookie center Alvan Adams and the team's leading scorer, ex-Celtics guard Paul Westphal.

The Suns had lost the first two games at the historic old Boston Garden but evened the series in

Phoenix. Now, back in Boston, they trailed by sixteen at halftime. They battled back, but it seemed they'd gone about as far as they could. Only fifty-five seconds to go, and they still trailed 95–90 with the wild Boston crowd on its feet and screaming for blood.

Then Suns guard Westphal went into action. Like a whirlwind, he sank a jump shot, and when the Celtics got the ball back, he stole it away and drove to the basket, inviting a foul. It was his only chance. He took his shot. In it went, and up went the referee's arm. Foul. Westphal stepped to the line. He shot again—and made it. Tie game.

Boston and Phoenix battled through the first over-time period, ending in a 101–101 deadlock. The crowd was roaring itself hoarse, but soon even more exciting action would take place. With just five seconds on the clock in the second overtime period, the Suns' Curtis Perry sank a long jump shot to put Phoenix up ahead, 110–109. Now it was Boston's turn for heroics—and jump shots. The Celtics' John Havlicek did the honors, putting his team up by a point. The buzzer sounded, and the wild beer-drinking crowd swarmed onto the floor.

Even though Boston had won, the crowd's mood was ugly. They attacked one referee and jostled the visiting Suns players. The Suns had to shove and push their way back to their locker room.

It would soon get worse. Another ref was signaling that the game wasn't over. Seeing the season going down the drain, Phoenix coach John MacLeod had called an illegal time-out when there was just one

A Ivan Adams was a vital part of the Suns' 1976 team. At the end of the season he was named rookie of the year for his efforts.

second left in the game. It was a desperate gamble to stop the clock, but it was the only move MacLeod had left on his coaching chessboard. Boston now had a foul shot.

It took ten minutes to clear the stunned and angry crowd off the court. Boston's Jo Jo White made the foul attempt. Now the Celtics were ahead by two, but Phoenix got to throw the ball back in from midcourt. Just before the buzzer blared again, the Suns' Gar Heard swished a long jumper. Triple overtime!

The crowd was now more incensed than ever. Garbage poured from the upper balconies onto the court. Fans ran onto the court. Boston police had to

The Garden Party

*M*oving with the ball, Paul Westphal is guarded by former Phoenix Sun Charlie Scott during the 1976 NBA Finals. The Celtics eventually won the series in six games.

break up several fights. While the action was hot in the stands, the Suns, no doubt drained by two near escapes from defeat, were cold. They should have held the advantage. Two key Celtics, center Dave Cowens and forward Paul Silas (later a Suns assistant coach), had fouled out, and Boston had to go to its bench. Celtics sub Glenn McDonald proved the key to the outcome, though. Everyone else—on the court and off—must have been drained, but McDonald scored 6 points, putting his team up by the same number of points with just 36 seconds left. It looked like Boston finally had it in the bag. The Suns came back with two quick baskets, but with twelve seconds remaining, Boston's Jo Jo White began dribbling away to eat up the clock.

Soon it was over. Boston had won. In the Celtics locker room, coach Tommy Heinsohn collapsed from the strain. Three days later, Boston clinched the finals. It was all over. Phoenix had distinguished themselves against basketball's traditional powerhouse—but they had also begun a frustrating pattern of shattered play-off dreams.

*E*yeing the basket, Dick Van Arsdale attempts to get past Jon McGlocklin of Milwaukee. Van Arsdale was a member of the first Phoenix Suns team.

2

BIRTH OF A TEAM

The Suns took their first step toward becoming part of the National Basketball Association on May 6, 1968, when the NBA held an expansion draft to staff the Suns and the other new team in the league, the Milwaukee Bucks. Most of the players these new teams had to choose from were of very low quality, but the Suns did get very lucky with Dick Van Arsdale, whom they selected from the New York Knicks. In Van Arsdale's first Phoenix season, he averaged 21 points. He remained with the Suns eight more years, averaging 17.6 points per game over his Phoenix career and making the NBA All-Star Game three times. In Dick's final NBA season (1976–77), his twin brother, Tom, joined the Suns, and the Van Arsdales became the first twins to be NBA teammates.

Dick Van Arsdale was clearly the good news for the expansion Suns, the only good news. The Suns' first season was a disaster, as they won just 16 games, while losing 66 for a .195 won-lost percentage—the worst record in the NBA.

Then things got worse. Ordinarily, such a dreadful record would guarantee a team the first pick in the next year's NBA draft. The NBA, however, had decided that the last-place teams in its two divisions would flip a coin to decide who would get first dibs in the draft. The Suns lost the coin toss—and the right to choose UCLA's Kareem Abdul-Jabbar, who would become one of the greatest superstars in NBA history.

The 1970s

Phoenix surprised everyone with their 1969–70 playoff appearance, but they soon sank back to the second division, not making the playoffs again until 1975–76, when they battled the Boston Celtics for the NBA Championship. Despite a losing record the following year, coach John MacLeod's Suns soon bounced back, making the playoffs every year from 1979 through 1985. The Suns were helped by two NBA Rookies of the Year, Alvan "Double A" Adams (1975–76) and Walter Davis (1977–78). When Davis joined with Paul Westphal, the Suns could easily claim the finest guard-forward combination in the National Basketball Association.

Other key Suns in that era were aggressive six-foot seven-inch forward/center Leonard "Truck" Robinson, who led NBA rebounders in 1977–78, and six-foot four-inch guard Dennis "DJ" Johnson, who came over

*C*onnie Hawkins (42) glides past Billy Cunningham (32) on his way to the basket. Hawkins and the Suns made the playoffs in only their second season as a franchise.

Kareem Abdul-Jabbar of the L.A. Lakers makes a pass over James Edwards (55) and Kyle Macy (4) of Phoenix. The Lakers and the Suns met in the 1984 Western Conference Finals.

from Seattle after squabbling with SuperSonics coach Lenny Wilkens. Six-foot ten-inch Larry Nance was taken in the 1981 draft. He later performed his awesome double dunks and power slams for Phoenix for six seasons.

After 1976, the Suns would not make the NBA Finals for several years, but they did return to post-season play the following season, losing to the Bucks 2–0 in the first round. In 1979, the high-scoring (115.5 points per game) Suns made it to the Western Conference Finals before falling to the Seattle SuperSonics in seven games.

The Phoenix Suns Basketball Team

The 1980s

In 1980, the Suns were beaten in the Western Conference Semifinals in five games, the first two of which they lost in overtime. The following year, Phoenix lost the semifinals in seven games to the Kansas City (now Sacramento) Kings. The Suns had rallied from a 3-1 deficit to tie the series. Their 95–88 loss in the decisive seventh game was particularly disappointing, because it came on the Suns' home court.

In 1982, Phoenix lost the semifinals to the Lakers in four straight, the first two games by twenty-one points each. In 1983, they were eliminated in the first round by Denver, but in 1984 they made it all the way to the Western Conference Finals before falling in six games to Coach Pat Riley's Los Angeles Lakers. The following year, the Lakers swept the Suns in the post-season's first round.

The Suns' poor playoff record was bad enough, but by the late 1980s they weren't even able to see any postseason play. Truck Robinson was traded to the Knicks, Alvan Adams retired, and five other Suns were accused of illegal drug use, although none was ever prosecuted or even disciplined by the NBA.

The team was in major need of rebuilding. Many thought it might even leave Phoenix. Few Suns fans could suspect that the team's greatest days were right around the corner.

*M*aintaining his coverage, Connie Hawkins looks to block Walt Frazier's shot. Hawkins scored 20 points a game in his first three years with the Suns.

TALENT TO SPARE

Many great players have worn a Phoenix Suns uniform. They've been remarkable individuals not only because of their on-court talent, but also because of their fascinating backgrounds and personalities.

Connie Hawkins

Although many said he was innocent, high school standout Connie Hawkins had been banned from NBA and college play after being linked to a gambling scandal. "One of the most promising careers in basketball history was seemingly over before it had even started," noted Dr. Peter Bjarkman in *The Encyclopedia of Pro Basketball*. Still, the American Basketball Association (ABA), a one-time rival of the NBA, gave Hawkins a chance to play, and Hawkins showed just how good he really was. He then sued the NBA to have the ban lifted. The NBA agreed that

Hawkins could play in their league, and the Suns jumped at the chance to sign him. Although he was near the end of his career, he averaged better than 20.0 points per game in his first three seasons with Phoenix.[1]

Alvan Adams

Alvan Adams was the first Phoenix Sun to be named NBA Rookie of the Year. The six-foot nine-inch center, who had starred with the University of Oklahoma's Sooners, played for the Suns for his entire thirteen-year pro career, helping them to the playoffs nine times. Adams's career game highs were 47 points and 19 rebounds.

Paul Westphal

Paul Westphal enjoyed a highly successful twelve NBA seasons, five of which he spent with the Suns. He had been a first-round draft pick of the Celtics, and played three years in Boston before being traded to Phoenix. The six-foot four-inch, 195 pound Westphal used a patented highly effective bank shot to lead the club in scoring each year, with his best mark being 25.2 points per game in 1989. He was "considered the best guard in the NBA" and four times made the NBA All-Star team. The Suns retired his uniform number (44) in 1989.[2]

Dan Majerle

Guard/forward Dan Majerle (MAR-LEE) played for Phoenix for seven seasons, beginning in 1988–89. He

The Phoenix Suns Basketball Team

*L*ooking very determined, Paul Westphal
dribbles past Tom Kropp of the Chicago Bulls.
The Suns retired Westphal's number in 1989.

eventually became one of the franchise's most popular
players, averaging 16 points per game and leading all
league guards in voting for the 1995 All-Star Game.
When he was first selected by Phoenix in the NBA
draft, though, Suns fans were angry that their team
had picked someone from a school as obscure as
Central Michigan. A Suns broadcaster phoned Majerle
and told him the fans were booing him in Phoenix. He
wanted to know how Majerle felt about that. It really
didn't matter what the fans thought right now, Majerle
responded; they had no idea who he actually was.

*C*harles Barkley reaches around Shawn Bradley of the New Jersey Nets to try to get to the hoop. Barkley was the first Sun to be named the league's MVP.

How right he was. Majerle won Suns fans over with his fearless, hard-driving style of play. Charles Barkley once commented, "Dan Majerle is just as tough as I am. There are not that many players in the league that tough."[3]

Charles Barkley

Of course, when it came to toughness and hard work, Suns superstar Charles Barkley knew what he was talking about.

In high school, Barkley wasn't particularly tall, but he worked hard on his jumping and became an excellent rebounder. In college, he had weight problems. Fans taunted him with names such as The Round Mound of Rebound. Once again, he went to work, and where there once was fat, there now was muscle.[4]

Barkley first became an exciting NBA presence with the Philadelphia 76ers, but he continued to excel with Phoenix, becoming the first Sun to win NBA Most Valuable Player honors. At his peak—despite his lack of height—he was regularly the only NBA player among the top five in both rebounding and scoring.

Barkley was also known for colorful in-your-face personality. He developed a reputation for making outrageous statements, regarding such on-court and off-court topics as becoming governor of Alabama, and even his personal life.

"Does your wife think you're good-looking?" he was once asked.

"No," he responded, "She thinks I've got $25 million."[5]

Jerry Colangelo (right), Suns president and part owner, presents a trophy to Paul Westphal (left). Colangelo became the Suns' first general manager at the age of twenty-eight.

OFF-COURT STARS

Many sports owners, such as the Yankees' George Steinbrenner or the Raiders' Al Davis, have very poor reputations, but that doesn't apply to the Phoenix Suns' Jerry Colangelo.

Jerry Colangelo: Three-Fourths Owner

Except for playing for the Suns, Colangelo has done just about everything else for them—and that includes even working out with the team and shooting baskets against the Suns for money.

At age twenty-eight, Colangelo became Phoenix's first general manager—the youngest GM in major-league sports history. Twice he stepped in to coach the team. In the late 1980s, the Suns were in deep trouble. Other clubs routinely defeated them—often by lop-sided scores. There were ugly rumors of drug use. It looked like Phoenix was about to lose its team. Colangelo stepped in, and in October 1988 he organized a group of local investors who purchased the franchise for $44.5 million.

Soon Colangelo was offered $60 million if he would move the team out of town. He said no and set about rebuilding the club—and keeping it in Phoenix. He did it without controversy and without sticking his nose into every detail of the Suns' operations. "The trick is knowing how to delegate," he once revealed. "The mistake a lot of CEOs [Chief Executive Officers] make is knowing a little about a lot of things—and getting too involved."[1]

"I think Jerry is the single biggest reason why Phoenix is a showcase franchise," says Danny Ainge, "why so many people want to come here. He's a guy who can be trusted and is well respected."[2]

It's no surprise that Colangelo has been named as *Sporting News* NBA Executive of the Year four times.

Red Kerr

The Sun's first coach was Johnny "Red" Kerr, a former center who grabbed over 10,000 rebounds in his NBA career and who later coached the Chicago Bulls. The six-foot nine-inch Kerr lasted for only two seasons.

John MacLeod

In 1973, Colangelo appointed John MacLeod as the Sun's coach. MacLeod had never played in the NBA (he is only six feet tall) but had been a successful college coach when Colangelo tapped him for the job. He became the Suns' longest lasting coach, leading

*J*ohn MacLeod took over as coach of the Phoenix Suns in 1973. MacLeod went on to coach the Suns for fourteen seasons until 1987.

them for a record fourteen seasons, including four fifty-plus win campaigns. As the team fell apart, MacLeod was fired in April 1987.

Cotton Fitzsimmons

Lowell "Cotton" Fitzsimmons, who had briefly coached the Suns years before, returned as coach for the 1988–89 season, and helped guide them back to respectability, taking them to the playoffs in each of his four Suns seasons and winning honors as 1988–89 NBA Coach of the Year. "He made us realize . . . ," said Kevin Johnson, "that we can win right now. He made us see a little further than we were willing to look."[3]

*A*fter his playing days were over, Phoenix brought Paul Westphal back to be the head coach. In his first year the Suns won 62 games which is still the club record.

Paul Westphal

When Colangelo hired Fitzsimmons, however, he also hired former Suns star Paul Westphal as one of Fitzsimmons's assistants. Colangelo planned that one day the younger Westphal would succeed Fitzsimmons. "It's a great opportunity for me," said Westphal, who was then coaching at Phoenix's Grand Canyon College.[4]

For the 1992–93 season, Westphal replaced Fitzsimmons as coach. Fitzsimmons stayed with the Suns, becoming Phoenix's executive vice president and a team broadcaster. With the addition of such stars as Charles Barkley and Kevin "K.J." Johnson, the Suns were ready to make their move toward an NBA championship. Westphal has managed many exciting players but is personally known for his low-key style. Oddly enough, during his playing days Westphal had a reputation for often questioning his coaches' decisions, particularly those of John MacLeod.

Westphal was an instant success. It took him just 140 games to record 100 NBA wins. Only Red Auerbach, Pat Riley, and Bill Russell did better. In Westphal's first season with the Suns, he won 62 games, the all-time record for a rookie NBA coach, and still the club season record for wins. He was also only the fifth rookie to coach in an NBA All-Star Game.

When the Suns stumbled in their 1995–96 season, Westphal lost his position. His replacement: Cotton Fitzsimmons.

Knifing through the defense, Dan Majerle looks for the easy lay-up. Phoenix started to build a championship caliber team by adding players such as Majerle and Kevin Johnson.

SUN-SHINE

n 1990–91, the Suns continued building their reputation for excellence—and consistency—again finishing third (behind the Trail Blazers and the Lakers) with a fine 55-27 mark. This time, the team did not fare as well in the postseason, getting blown away, 4–0, in the first round by Karl Malone's Utah Jazz.

By now the Suns must have felt they were in a rut—good enough to be ranked among the top teams in the NBA, but not good enough to be the best either in the NBA or even in their division. Once more they finished third, this time behind Portland and Golden State, with a 53-29 record. In the playoff's first round they demolished David Robinson and the San Antonio Spurs in three straight games, yet San Antonio wouldn't go down without a struggle. In game three, the Spurs—helped by consecutive three-pointers by Sean Elliot and Trent Tucker—pulled within five points, with 4:40 on the clock. Then, with just thirty-five seconds left, San Antonio cut Phoenix's margin to just three points.

That was as close as the Spurs got, as the Suns came alive and poured it on in the clutch. San Antonio never scored again, and Phoenix won, 101–92.

Then, in the Semifinals, reality again reared its ugly head. Portland eclipsed the Suns, 4–1, although the Trailblazers had to take Phoenix into double overtime in game four, to beat them, 153–151.

A Dramatic Change

Jerry Colangelo and Cotton Fitzsimmons felt that something dramatic had to be done in order for the Suns to rise above the rest of the Pacific Division. In the entire NBA, there was nothing more dramatic than the Sixers' bald-headed, trash-talking monster rebounder, Charles Barkley. The Suns traded for him. For once the brash Barkley was almost speechless. "Words cannot express how happy I feel right now," said Barkley. "This is my best chance to win a championship."[1]

To obtain Sir Charles, Phoenix had to surrender three of their key players—All-Star guard Jeff Hornacek, starting forward Tim Perry, and backup center Andrew Lang—but it was worth it. The next season, the rebuilt Suns posted a franchise-record 62 victories, the best in the entire NBA as Barkley captured MVP honors and six-foot seven-inch forward Cedric "Ice" Ceballos led the NBA with his .576 field goal percentage.

Division championships and awards were not enough for Barkley and the Suns. They had bigger

Kevin Johnson steals the ball from Portland's Buck Williams and heads up court. The Suns faced the Trailblazers in the second round of the 1992 playoffs.

things in mind. "Our goal is to get three of them [NBA championship banners]," Barkley boasted after clinching first in the regular season, "and you don't get all three unless you get the first one. We didn't come here just to win the Pacific Division. At least, I didn't."[2]

It certainly looked like this powerhouse team might finally go all the way, as they went 14-0 to begin the 1992–93 season and steamrollered their way into the NBA finals. However, superstar Michael Jordan and the Chicago Bulls, a team coming off two straight NBA Championships, stood in Phoenix's path.

The Suns gave it their best. In Game 3, just as in the classic Game 5 of the 1975 Finals, Phoenix went

Sun-Shine

Determined to get the bucket, Kevin Johnson shoots over the Bulls' Michael Jordan. In 1993, Phoenix played the Chicago Bulls for the NBA Championship.

into triple overtime. This time the Suns were the winners, beating the Bulls in Chicago, 129–121.

With just 3.9 seconds remaining in the series's final game, veteran Chicago guard John Paxson launched a last-ditch three-pointer, to put his team ahead by a single point. The Suns' Kevin Johnson retaliated with a desperate drive to the basket, but Bulls forward Horace Grant blocked his layup. The game ended as a thrilling 99–98 Bulls victory, making Chicago "three-peat" NBA champions. The Phoenix Suns slunk home, disappointed once more.

This Could Be the Year

The biggest news of 1993 in basketball, in perhaps all of sports, was Michael Jordan's retirement. The Suns had just lost out to Jordan and his teammates and were poised to move upward. Phoenix thought it could win it all the following season, 1993–94. Instead, they finished second to Seattle in the Pacific Division and fell to Nigerian-born Hakeem Olajuwon and the Houston Rockets in the Western Conference Semifinals.

The 1994–95 Suns were beset with injuries. Charles Barkley missed the first eleven games of the season, but came back to be the key man in Coach Paul West-phal's always changing lineup. Kevin Johnson missed thirty-five contests with a variety of leg problems. Forward Danny Manning injured his left knee in early February and missed the rest of the season. Still, the Suns managed to capture the Pacific Division for the second time in three years, but fell to Houston in the conference semifinals in seven games after leading the series, 3–1, in the first four games.

In full stride, Danny Manning looks to blow past Rasheed Wallace of the Bullets. The Suns hope that Manning is one of the players that will lead them back to the NBA Finals.

A SUNNY FORECAST

t's never easy to predict the future of any sports franchise, but the Phoenix Suns may be an exception to that rule. The Suns may or may not win an NBA championship. They may or may not make the playoffs. They may even have a losing season for a year or two. One thing can be said about Phoenix, though. With Jerry Colangelo and his management team in charge, the Suns will remain one of the NBA's most stable and respected operations.

New Talent

That reputation has resulted in real benefits for the Suns. In the 1994–95 season, both Danny Manning and Wayman Tisdale rejected much larger contracts to perform with Phoenix. Manning settled for $1 million to play with the Suns. He could have earned $5 million elsewhere. Tisdale, previously with the

Sacramento Kings, rejected a $3 million offer from the Los Angeles Clippers to sign with the Suns for "just" $850,000.

"Danny Manning and Wayman Tisdale signing the contracts they did are great stories," said Colangelo. "They're great stories because in this day and age of salaries and greed, it's great to see a couple of men of character and talent totally prioritize differently. [They were] willing to play on a one-year basis so that they can play with our organization, with our team, in our city. Money was way down the list."[1]

That may not have been exactly true. Both Tisdale and Manning were also playing the economics of the NBA's salary cap. After signing one-year Phoenix contracts, they could gain even more money as unrestricted free agents. Still, they didn't have to go to Phoenix—but they did.

Colangelo also uses very subtle—but very effective—techniques of player recruitment. When the Suns were trying to sign the Los Angeles Lakers' A.C. Green, the club owner escorted him into the Phoenix locker room. Hanging in a locker, just waiting for the durable six-foot nine-inch, 225-pound forward was a Suns uniform with his name on it. For extra effect, a spotlight shone upon it, hitting the garment at just the right angle. The message was unmistakable: Sign with Phoenix, and be a star.

Green signed for $1.9 million. The following year, he agreed to a five-year $5 million Suns contract.

Dan Majerle was a mainstay of the Phoenix Suns. In 1995, however, he was traded to the Cleveland Cavaliers.

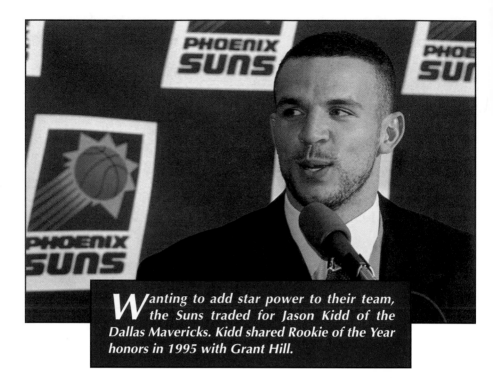

Wanting to add star power to their team, the Suns traded for Jason Kidd of the Dallas Mavericks. Kidd shared Rookie of the Year honors in 1995 with Grant Hill.

Hometown Favorites

Symbolic of the Suns' popularity in Phoenix is their new home: the $90 million, 19,023-seat America West Arena, which opened on November 7, 1992. Before the America West Arena opened, the Suns played in Phoenix's Arizona Veterans' Memorial Coliseum, one of the oldest arenas in the NBA. Colangelo was determined that the Suns' new home court would be a source of pride. The America West Arena boasts a food court for fans, four parking garages, and locker rooms big enough to house forty-five players each (there are only twelve players on an NBA roster).

The Phoenix Suns Basketball Team

The Suns have also reached out to Arizona's large Native American population. In 1993, Phoenix became the first NBA team to broadcast a game in Navajo. The announcer, Kenneth Maryboy, used ancient words in the Navajo language to compare players to coyotes or legendary monster slayers.

Rebuilding Again

When the 1995–96 season began, the Suns looked like an aging team—and a bad one. Their play was so bad that Jerry Colangelo replaced Paul Westphal with former Suns coach Cotton Fitzsimmons.

Fitzsimmons began playing younger players. With five rookies (Mario Bennett, Chris Carr, John Coker, Michael Finley, and Terrence Rencher) on the Suns roster, only the expansion Toronto Raptors could boast as many first-year players.

The Suns ended the 1995–96 season, 41-41, fourth in the Pacific Division. After being eliminated in the first round of the playoffs, Phoenix decided to make some off-the-court moves. Charles Barkley was traded to Houston for Sam Cassell, Robert Horry, Mark Bryant, and Chucky Brown.

As the season got underway it became obvious that this Suns team would need further changes. In a series of trades the Suns parted with Cassell, Horry, Finley, and A.C. Green, while receiving all-stars Jason Kidd and Cedric Ceballos. With the addition of these star players the Suns look to rise to the top of the league once more.

STATISTICS

Team Record

SEASON	SEASON RECORD	PLAYOFF RECORD	COACH	DIVISION FINISH
1968–69	16-66	—	John Kerr	7th
1969–70	39-43	3-4	John Kerr/ Jerry Colangelo	3rd
1970–71	48-34	—	Cotton Fitzsimmons	3rd
1971–72	49-33	—	Cotton Fitzsimmons	3rd
1972–73	38-44	—	Jerry Colangelo/ Bill van Breda Kolff	3rd
1973–74	30-52	—	John MacLeod	4th
1974–75	32-50	—	John MacLeod	4th
1975–76	42-40	10-9	John MacLeod	3rd
1976–77	34-48	—	John MacLeod	5th
1977–78	49-33	0-2	John MacLeod	2nd
1978–79	50-32	9-6	John MacLeod	2nd
1979–80	55-27	3-5	John MacLeod	3rd
1980–81	57-25	3-4	John MacLeod	1st
1981–82	46-36	2-5	John MacLeod	3rd
1982–83	53–29	1-2	John MacLeod	2nd
1983–84	41-41	9-8	John MacLeod	4th
1984–85	36-46	0-3	John MacLeod	3rd
1985–86	32-50	—	John MacLeod	3rd
1986–87	36-46	—	John MacLeod/ Dick Van Arsdale	5th
1987–88	28-54	—	John Wetzel	4th
1988–89	55-27	7-5	Cotton Fitzsimmons	2nd
1989–90	54-28	9-7	Cotton Fitzsimmons	3rd
1990–91	55-27	1-3	Cotton Fitzsimmons	3rd
1991–92	53-29	4-4	Cotton Fitzsimmons	3rd

The Phoenix Suns Basketball Team

Team Record (con't)

SEASON	SEASON RECORD	PLAYOFF RECORD	COACH	DIVISION FINISH
1992–93	62-20	13-11	Paul Westphal	1st
1993–94	56-26	6-4	Paul Westphal	2nd
1994–95	59-23	6-4	Paul Westphal	2nd
1995–96	41-41	1-3	Paul Westphal/ Cotton Fitzsimmons	4th
Totals	1246-1050	87-89		

Coaching Records

COACH	SEASONS	RECORD	CHAMPIONSHIPS
John Kerr	1968–70	31-89	None
Jerry Colangelo	1969–70 1972–73	59-60	None
Cotton Fitzsimmons	1970–72 1988–92 1995–96	341-200	None
Bill van Breda Kolff	1972–73	3-4	None
John MacLeod	1973–87	579-543	1980–81 Pacific Division
Dick Van Arsdale	1986–87	14-12	None
John Wetzel	1987–88	28-54	None
Paul Westphal	1992–96	191-88	1992–93 Pacific Division

Ten Greatest Suns

PLAYER	SEA	YRS	G	CAREER STATISTICS					
				REB	AST	BLK	STL	PTS	AVG
Alvan Adams	1975–88	13	988	6,937	4,012	808	1,289	13,910	14.1
Charles Barkley	1992–96	12	890	10,311	3,495	818	1,451	20,740	23.3
Tom Chambers	1988–93	14	1,094	6,687	2,279	627	882	20,024	18.3
Connie Hawkins	1969–73	7	499	3,971	2,052	—	—	8,233	16.5
Jeff Hornacek	1986–92	10	790	2,793	4,177	155	1,185	11,789	14.9
Jason Kidd	1996–	2	160	983	1,390	50	326	2,270	14.2
Dan Majerle	1988–95	8	612	2,952	1,948	277	844	8,606	14.1
Danny Manning	1994–	8	478	2,987	1,436	512	673	8,792	18.4
Dick Van Arsdale	1968–77	12	921	3,807	3,060	—	—	15,079	16.4
Paul Westphal	1975–80	12	823	1,580	3,591	—	—	12,809	15.6

SEA=Seasons with Suns
YRS=Years in the NBA
G=Games

REB=Rebounds
AST=Assists
BLK=Blocks

STL=Steals
PTS=Total Points
AVG=Scoring Average

The Phoenix Suns Basketball Team

CHAPTER NOTES

Chapter 3

1. Dr. Peter C. Bjarkman, *The Encyclopedia of Pro Basketball* (New York: Carroll & Graf, 1994), p. 256

2. Martin Taragano, *Basketball Biographies* (Jefferson, N.C.: McFarland & Co., 1991), p. 295.

3. Darryl Howerton, "Majerle Hustle," *Sport*, January 1994, pp. 47–49.

4. Glen Macnow, *Sports Great Charles Barkley* (Springfield, N.J.: Enslow Publishers, Inc, 1992), p. 20.

5. Leigh Montville, "He's Everywhere," *Sports Illustrated*, May 3, 1993, pp. 78–82.

Chapter 4

1. William II. Miller, "Jerry Colangelo's Palace in the Sun," *Industry Week*, April 6, 1992.

2. Kevin Simpson, "The Place to Be," *The Sporting News*, November 7, 1994.

3. Bruce Newman, "Risen Again," *Sports Illustrated*, February 7, 1989, p. 38

4. "Fitzsimmons to Coach Suns, Groom Westphal," *Washington Post*, May 11, 1988

Chapter 5

1. Glen Macnow, *Sports Great Charles Barkley* (Springfield, N.J.: Enslow Publishers, Inc, 1992), p. 61.

2. David DuPree, "Suns Burn Jazz 112–99, Win Division," *USA Today*, April 12, 1993, p. 1C.

Chapter 6

1. Kevin Simpson, "The Place to Be," *The Sporting News*, November 7, 1994.

GLOSSARY

American Basketball Association—A rival to the National Basketball Association. It operated from 1967 to 1976. Four of its teams, the New York Nets, Indiana Pacers, San Antonio Spurs, and Denver Nuggets, became members of the NBA.

dribbling—Moving the ball down the court by repeatedly bouncing it.

field goal—A successful shot taken from the field. Usually called a basket.

field goal percentage—The number of successful field goals made divided by the number attempted.

foul—Illegal physical contact against an opposing player. The ball may then be given to the fouled player's team and/or a free throw (or foul shot).

jump shot—A shot taken after a player has jumped straight up in the air.

period—Each NBA game is divided into four twelve-minute periods.

overtime—The additional period or periods called for if a game is tied at the end of regulation play. Regulation periods are twelve minutes each; overtime periods are five minutes each.

rebound—Grabbing the ball off the backboard after a missed shot. An offensive rebound is taken off the opposing team's basket or backboard; a defensive rebound is taken off the team's own basket or backboard.

The Phoenix Suns Basketball Team

swish—A shot that goes through the basket without hitting the backboard or the rim.

technical foul—Unlike other fouls, a technical foul does not involve physical contact with an opposing player and can be assessed not only against players active in a game, but also against coaches or players on the bench.

time-out—A ninety-second halt in play. During a time-out, the clock is stopped.

FURTHER READING

Anderson, Dave. *The Story of Basketball.* New York: William Morrow & Co., 1988.

Bjarkman, Peter C. *The Encyclopedia of Pro Basketball: Team Histories.* New York: Carol & Graf, 1994.

Hollander, Zander, ed. *The Complete Handbook of Pro Basketball: 1996 Edition.* New York: Signet, 1995.

Macnow, Glen. *Sports Great Charles Barkley.* Springfield, N.J.: Enslow Publishers, 1992.

Official NBA Guide: 1995–96 Edition. St. Louis: The Sporting News, 1995.

Sachare, Alex, ed. *The Official NBA Basketball Encyclopedia, 2nd edition.* New York: Villard Books, 1994.

Sullivan, George. *This Is Pro Basketball.* New York: Dodd, Mead & Co., 1977.

Taragano, Martin. *Basketball Biographies.* Jefferson, N.C.: MacFarland & Co., 1991.

INDEX

WHERE TO WRITE

Phoenix Suns
201 E. Jefferson
Phoenix, AZ 85004

WEBSITE

http://www.nba.com/suns/